Cao Chong Weighs an Elephant

by Songju Ma Daemicke
illustrated by Christina Wald

Nearly two thousand years ago, in ancient China, there was a boy named Cao Chong who was curious and loved asking questions. He wondered if fish had ears, whether they could hear, and how they slept in the water.

One day, Chong was very excited because he was going to see a gigantic animal called an elephant. There had not been an elephant in their country before. It was a birthday present to his father Cao Cao, the Prime Minister of Han, from the emperor of the Wu Kingdom.

In the great courtyard outside the palace, the ambassador of the Wu Kingdom guided a huge, grey beast toward the anxiously waiting Cao Cao, his advisors, and hundreds of guests.

The enormous elephant used its long trunk to take one small nut at a time to its mouth from the hand of the ambassador. People applauded with delight.

Chong couldn't resist running directly up to the elephant to stroke its head. The playful elephant gently caressed him back with its long trunk, causing Chong to squeal with laughter.

"What a wonderful nose it has!" Chong said excitedly. "It works like an arm and a hand!"

One spectator remarked, "This elephant is magnificent! It must weigh five thousand jin!" Another declared, "With legs as thick as logs and feet as big as stumps, I think it must weigh at least six thousand jin!"

Excitedly joining in this guessing game, one advisor tried to measure the dimensions of the elephant. Another tried to lift one of the elephant's legs. The elephant patiently rolled its eyes and helped itself to more nuts directly from Chong's hands.

An advisor excitedly took a piece of jade from his belt. "I am willing to bet the weight of the elephant against my favorite piece of jade. Seven thousand jin!"

Another shouted, "I wager a weight of eight thousand jin against my best silver cup!"

An amused Cao Cao turned to the Wu ambassador. "Do you know exactly how much this elephant weighs?"

"No, my honorable Prime Minister," he replied. "Elephants are too big and heavy for our scales. Surely the wise people in your kingdom have a way to measure this."

Cao Cao winked at his advisors and smiled. "This elephant is not only a birthday present, but also a challenge to the intelligence and power of our country and its people."

He stood up. "My learned advisors and guests, who can tell me a way to determine exactly this elephant's weight?"

A quiet yet furious brainstorm now replaced the previous bold declarations.

One advisor finally suggested, "Perhaps we could build an extremely large scale, one large enough to hold an elephant!"

"Our scales are good for weighing food and small objects, but this animal is far too huge!" another said.

Yet another added, "The arms of the elephant scale would have to be enormous. The measuring pan itself would have to be as big as the floor of a small room."

Another voice cried out, "The mass would have to be as large as our biggest bronze bell!"

"Even if we could build a scale that large, how could we make the elephant stay still and balance on it?" scoffed another.

"Perhaps we could slice the elephant into smaller pieces to fit on a normal-sized scale," suggested a voice in the back of the crowd.

"What? Nonsense! That idea is totally silly and cruel!" someone scolded.

"You should not have to kill the elephant just to know its weight!" Chong spoke out in a serious tone. Many nodded in agreement.

"Father," Chong then called out. "I have a way!"

Cao Cao smiled. "You, my small boy, have a better method than all my wisest advisors?"

Chong ran back and whispered his idea directly into his father's ear.

Cao Cao's eyes brightened. "Yes! I think that will work! "

Chong, his father, and the guests
proceeded to a lake. A wooden boat
was moored next to the bank.

Chong led the elephant onto the boat. The weight of the elephant made the boat sink noticeably in the water. Chong directed the servants to use their knives to carve a line on the outside of the boat marking the water line.

Chong then guided the elephant off the boat and back to the land. The carved lines on the boat could be seen to rise again higher above the water.

One advisor seemed puzzled. "The elephant was put on the boat and now is taken off the boat. Little boy, what game are you playing here?"

"You will see." Chong smiled confidently.

Chong then ordered that rocks be loaded into the boat. The boat started to sink back lower into the water again.

A few advisors now understood and opened their eyes wide with sudden amazement. "What a clever idea!"

When the long, curved line on the boat again met the water's surface, Chong hopped back on the boat. He waved his hands. "Stop! Now bring a scale and weigh all the rocks on this boat!"

The servants cried out the readings to Chong,

"45 jin!"

"36 jin!"

"53 jin!"

"72 jin!"

"Don't forget me!" Chong shouted, hopping on the scale to be weighed.

"Chong weighs 49 jin."

Chong combined the weights of all the stones and subtracted his own weight. He proudly announced, "Father, the elephant weighs exactly nine thousand, three hundred, ninety eight (9398) jin!"

Loud applause and cheers burst out from the impressed crowd.

"Bravo!"

"Clever!"

"Ingenious!"

"What a smart boy!"

The elephant also seemed pleased, raising its trunk, blowing water into the air, and trumpeting a thunderous roar of approval.

Beaming with pride and satisfaction, Cao Cao embraced Chong into his arms. "Good thinking, my son! By solving the riddle of the elephant's weight, you have proved our intelligence not only to the Wu Kingdom, but also to the whole world!"

For Creative Minds

Sink or Float: Understanding Buoyancy

If you put a rock in the bathtub, it sinks. If you put a rubber duck in the tub, it floats—even if the rock and the boat weigh the same amount. Why?

Buoyancy is a force in liquids. It pushes objects up. Gravity pulls objects down. When you put a rock or a rubber duck on the surface of the water, it will sink or float depending on which force is stronger. The force of buoyancy changes depends on the weight of the liquid and the weight of the object.

If you fill a cup all the way to the very top and then put a rock in it, some of the water spills over. The water that spills over is **displaced**. It is pushed out of the way by the rock. That water has the same **volume** as the rock. It takes up the same amount of space in the cup. If you weigh the water that spilled and weigh the rock, you will see that the rock weighs more. Although they are the same volume, the rock is more **dense**. (Archimedes' principle)

The force of buoyancy is the same as the weight of the displaced liquid. Because the rock is heavier than the force pushing up against it, the rock sinks through the water. If you put a rubber duck in a very full bowl of water, will the duck weigh more or less than the water that is displaced?

Hands-on Learning

You will need:
- a cup
- warm water
- an egg
- salt
- a spoon

Fill the cup halfway with warm water. Place the egg in the cup.

Does the egg sink or float?

Add a spoonful of salt and stir until it dissolves. Be gentle stirring with the egg in the cup. If the glass is too small, take the egg out and put it back in after the salt dissolves.

Has anything changed? Add another spoonful of salt. Stir until it dissolves.

Continue adding salt one spoonful at a time and dissolving it in the water.

Does anything change as you add more salt?

What is the difference between fresh water and salt water?

How does that difference affect the force of buoyancy acting on the egg?

What do you think will happen if you add more fresh water to fill the rest of the cup?

Try it and see! What happens? Were you right?

Using Scales

How much does an elephant weigh? How much does a car weigh? How much do you weigh? How do you know?

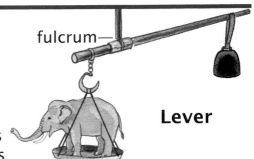

fulcrum—

Lever

A **scale** is a tool used to weigh things. It measures gravity's pull on an object.

Today, scales are common, high-tech devices. Modern scales provide very accurate measures almost instantly. But this has not always been the case.

A mechanical scale uses a simple machine, a **lever**, to compare two weights. A lever is a rod that pivots (turns) on a fixed point, called the **fulcrum**. One side of the scale holds a known weight, called the reference weight. The other side holds the object being measured.

You can find the weight of the object by changing the reference weight. You can add or remove reference weights until the lever balances out. Or you can move the reference weight along the lever. The farther a weight is from the fulcrum, the more **force** it has. Like an adult and a child on a seesaw, the scale can balance out when the lighter weight is farther from the fulcrum.

Chong used a mechanical scale and the principal of buoyancy to weigh an elephant. He put the elephant on a boat and marked the water level. Then the servants filled the boat with rocks until it sank to the same line as when the elephant was on it. They weighed each rock and Chong added the weights together. These rocks combined weighed the same as the elephant, because they both made the boat sink to the same level in the water.

Today, elephants are weighed on giant, digital scales.

This scale measures weight in pounds. Callee weighs 7825 pounds. This is the same as 3549 kg or 7098 jin.

Does Callee weigh more or less than the elephant in this story?

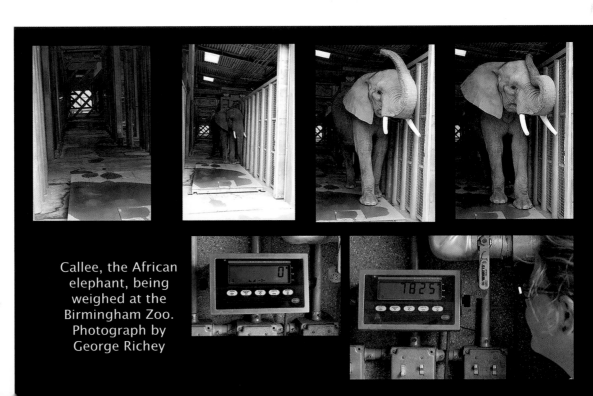

Callee, the African elephant, being weighed at the Birmingham Zoo. Photograph by George Richey

Cao Chong in History

Cao Chong was born in 196 AD, near the end of the Han Dynasty. By the time Chong was five years old, people said he was as smart as an adult. When an elephant arrived as a gift from the Wu Kingdom, Chong used the principal of buoyancy to weigh the large animal.

Chong's father, Cao Cao, was the chancellor (another word for Prime Minister) of Han. The emperor at this time, Emperor Xian, was a young man. Cao Cao ruled in the young emperor's name, but never tried to take the title of "emperor" for himself.

After Cao Cao died in 220, the Han Empire split into three kingdoms. These were the Wei Kingdom, the Wu Kingdom, and the Shu Kingdom. Seventy years later, a historian named Chen Shou wrote the story of Chong and the elephant in his history book, called the *Records of the Three Kingdoms*.

Cao Chong's name is sometimes written as Chong Cao. His given name is Chong, and his family name is Cao. A given name is the name that refers to one individual person within a family. A family name, also called a surname, is shared by people in the family to show that they are related. In Chinese tradition, the family name comes first and then the given name. In American tradition, the given name (first name) is followed by the family name (last name).

What is your given name? What is your family name?

Things to think about:

1. Is Cao Chong a historical figure or a fictional character?
2. How long ago did Cao Chong live?
3. How do you think Chong's life was different from yours?
4. How do you think Chong's life was similar to yours?
5. Do you and Chong have anything in common?
6. Have you ever come up with a solution for a problem? What was the problem? How did you solve it?

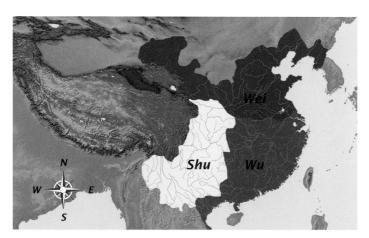

Three Kingdoms, 220 AD

On June 1, 2008, International Children's Day, the Chinese government issued stamps to celebrate Cao Chong, the child who figured out how to weigh an elephant.

Geography: China Then and Now

These maps show Han (red) in 200 AD and China (white) in 2000 AD.

A coordinate grid is a tool used to locate a specific place on the map. A letter and number together point to a single square on the map. For example, D9 shows the southern part of the Korean peninsula. Today this is the country of South Korea. Use the coordinate grid on the maps below to answer the following questions.

1. Which is larger, Han in 200 AD or China in 2000 AD?

2. Where is Chang'an?

3. Where is Luoyang?

4. On this map, one square is approximately 250 miles on each side. In 190, the young Emperor Xian moved from Luoyang to Chang'an. About how far did he go?

5. Chang'an still exists today, although it has a different name. What is Chang'an called in modern China?

6. Shule was part of a major trade route called the "Silk Road." This trade connected ancient China and ancient Europe. What is the modern name for this city?

7. Was Shule part of Han in 200 AD?

8. Modern China is formally called the People's Republic of China. The capitol is Beijing. Where is Beijing?

9. What was Beijing called in Han?

10. Which city is north of Luoyang?

11. Which of these four cities has the same name that it had in 200 AD?

12. Which city is to the west of Beijing?

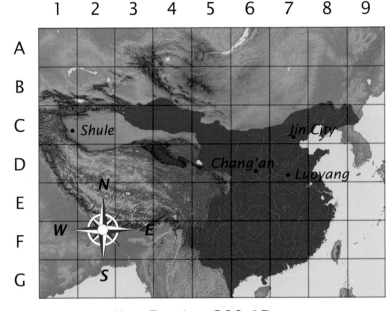

Han Empire, 200 AD

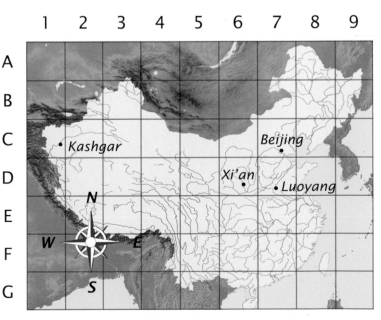

People's Republic of China, 2000 AD

Answers: 1) China. 2) D6. 3) D7. 4) 250 miles. 5) Xi'an. 6) Kashgar. 7) no. 8) C7. 9) Jin City. 10) Jin City/Beijing. 11) Luoyang. 12) Kashgar.

I dedicate this book to my husband, Dale, and to my three daughters, Feifei, Allison and Kathryn.—SMD

For everyone who strives to make the world a better place through peace and understanding.—CW

Thanks to Tammy Spicer, Director of Operations at Discovery Gateway: The Children's Museum of Utah, for verifying the accuracy of the buoyancy information in the For Creative Minds section.

Cataloging Information is available through the Library of Congress.

Library of Congress Cataloging in Publication Control Number: 2017019672

978-1-628559033   English hardcover
978-1-628559040   English paperback
978-1-628559057   Spanish paperback
978-1-628559064   English ebook downloadable
978-1-628559071   Spanish ebook downloadable
Interactive, read-aloud ebook featuring selectable English (978-1-628559088) and Spanish (978-1-628559095) text and audio (web and iPad/tablet based)

Translated into Spanish: ***Cao Chong pesa un elefante***

Lexile® Level: 830L
key phrases: buoyancy, China, measurement, scale, weight, historical figure

Bibliography:
"Cao Chong Weighing an Elephant." Cultural China. N.p., n.d. Web. 30 Jan. 2017.
Editors of Encyclopædia Britannica. "Archimedes' principle." Encyclopædia Britannica. Encyclopædia Britannica, inc., 08 Jan. 2016. Web. 24 Jan. 2017.
Farndon, John. Buoyancy. Tarrytown, NY: Benchmark , 2003. Print.
Idema, Wilt L., and Stephen H. West. Records of the Three Kingdoms in plain language. Indianapolis: Hackett Publishing Company, Inc, 2016. Print.

Text Copyright 2017 © by Songju Ma Daemicke
Illustration Copyright 2017 © by Christina Wald

The "For Creative Minds" educational section may be copied by the owner for personal use or by educators using copies in classroom settings

Manufactured in China, June 2017
This product conforms to CPSIA 2008
First Printing

Arbordale Publishing
Mt. Pleasant, SC 29464
www.ArbordalePublishing.com